WHAT YOU NEED TO KNOW ABOUT GANGS

by Lauri S. Friedman

Content Adviser:
Billy AraJeJe Woods, Ph.D.,
Department of Psychology, Saddleback College,
Mission Viejo, California

Reading Adviser:
Alexa L. Sandmann, Ed.D.,
Professor of Literacy, College and Graduate School
of Education, Health, and Human Services,
Kent State University

Compass Point Books
151 Good Counsel Drive
P.O. Box 669
Mankato, MN 56002-0669

 This book was manufactured with paper containing
at least 10 percent post-consumer waste.

Photographs ©: Karon Dubke/Capstone Press, cover, 29; iStockphoto/
kevinruss, cover (background), 17; Shutterstock/Jack Dagley Photography, 5, 6;
Jason Stitt, 11; Sasha Burkard, 12, 25; Joseph, 14; Bobby Deal/RealDealPhoto,
22; emin kuliyev, 24; Lisa F. Young, 27; Dan Lee, 32; Renata Fedosova, 34;
Ljupco Smokovski, 39; Getty Images Inc./Robert Nickelsberg, 7; AP Images/
Houston Chronicle, Steve Campbell, 10; Newscom, 15, 20, 40; Gloria Ferniz/
Express News, 30; Paul L. Richards/AFP/Getty Images, 31; Paul Hu/*Long Beach
Press Telegram*, 35; Joe Burbank/Orlando Sentinel, 38; Bruce Chambers, *The
Orange County Register*, 42; Bob Pepping/Contra Costa Times, 43.

Editor: Brenda Haugen
Page Production: Ashlee Suker
Photo Researcher: Marcie Spence
Art Director: LuAnn Ascheman-Adams
Creative Director: Joe Ewest
Editorial Director: Nick Healy
Managing Editor: Catherine Neitge

Library of Congress Cataloging-in-Publication Data
Friedman, Lauri S.
  Dangerous dues : what you need to know about gangs / by Lauri S.
Friedman ; content adviser: Billy AraJeJe Woods ; reading adviser: Alexa
L. Sandmann.
      p. cm.—(What's the issue?)
Includes bibliographical references and index.
ISBN 978-0-7565-4253-5 (library binding)
1. Gangs—United States—Juvenile literature. I. Woods, Billy
AraJeJe. II. Sandmann, Alexa L. III. Title. IV. Series.
HV6439.U5F75 2010
364.106'60973—dc22   2009006856

Visit Compass Point Books on the Internet at *www.compasspointbooks.com*
or e-mail your request to *custserv@compasspointbooks.com*

TABLE OF CONTENTS

CHAPTER one

GOING GANGSTA: THE DRAW OF GANGS FOR TEENAGERS

Gang life is a reality for nearly a million kids in the United States. Young people become gang members for many reasons. Some seek to fill a void that exists in their lives. Others view gangs as replacement families.

Others are drawn to them to feel respected and powerful. However, being part of a gang introduces a whole new world filled with crime, violence, and a lifetime of consequences—such as time in prison—or even death. The consequences of joining a gang far outweigh any perceived benefits, such as making money or gaining the respect of one's peers.

Gangs Feel Like Family

The Violence Prevention Institute found that people who join gangs tend to do so from the ages of 13 to 21. This is when vulnerable teens might give up hope that their

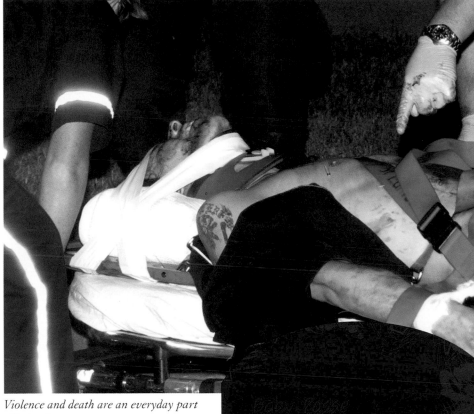

Violence and death are an everyday part of being in a gang.

families will take an interest in them. Take George,* a gang member in Houston, Texas. George explains how gangs fill in for family: "Let's say you have two parents who are working full-time jobs, and you can't even manage to survive, and then you have nobody around you to help and stuff. A gang's gonna end up

Kids as young as 8 years old can join gangs. It sounds crazy, but it's true. Sometimes they are the children or younger siblings of older gang members who are born into the lifestyle. More often, though, it's a neighborhood thing. Take the Fruit Belt Posse in Buffalo, New York, for example. This gang got its start in playgroups and schoolyards in one Buffalo neighborhood back in the 1980s. Its youngest members are called the Baby Posse.

* This and other names in this book have been changed for privacy reasons, except when reported in the media.

In a survey of more than 2,500 law enforcement agencies, 95 percent said gangs were active in their high schools. Ninety-one percent reported gang activities in their middle schools.

being like your family, helping you and keeping you company." George adds that gangs are there to "kick it with on weekends and at barbeques and stuff."

Teenagers like George who don't get enough attention from their families turn to gangs when they feel disconnected and lonely, says family therapist Tina Mears. For a kid whose family is absent, unsupportive, or abusive, fellow gangbangers seem more dependable than actual family members. To recruit members, gangs show more interest in the teen, making him or her feel that the gang is a family. Once a teen joins the gang, however, he or she quickly learns that a gang is actually a dangerous group of criminals that deals, steals, and murders to support its highest-ranking members.

The need to connect with others leads some teens to seek out gangs, while others end up in gangs by default. And with more than 24,500 gangs operating in the United States, it's easy for kids to get sucked in. Julia says she felt that she was expected to join the neighborhood gang. Last year six people in her neighborhood were killed in drive-by shootings. Julia says the violence was a message to local teens that joining one of the two

After investigating complaints of a loud party and drunken behavior, gang unit officers lined up members of the Crips street gang for body searches.

neighborhood gangs was mandatory. "That's how they do—you join or you pay," she says. "It's just expected in our neighborhood. After them people was shot, me, my brother, and our cousins all joined up. We had to. It was time."

Hugo was just 8 years old when his older brother Oscar—a member of the Oakland, California, Norteños gang—brought him along to meetings and parties so he would not be home alone. Both of their parents were in prison for gang-related offenses, so Oscar and the Norteños took care of Hugo. He remembers thinking: "The Norteños were everything to me. They were there for me when my parents was locked up. They were all my brothers. There was no question I would join [the gang]. I was always one of them cuz my brother was." Hugo and others are attracted to gangs because it feels good to be welcomed, accepted, and included by a group—even when that group is as dangerous as a gang.

Power and Respect

Gangs rule with fear in cities and towns both big and small—but the larger the city, the more powerful the gang. For example, gang violence is a problem for all U.S. cities with more than 250,000 people. Because they are part of an organization that can scare and hurt other people, gang members often feel powerful and respected. A former gang member known as Big Mike says: "Rollin' with my brothers was like insta-respect, man. You seen the fear in people's eyes when we was on the street. They just like, moved aside to let us go by." Gang members usually think that if others fear them, they will earn respect, says therapist Tina Mears.

Big Mike sought the respect and power offered by gang life

Since 1995 the National Youth Gang Center has been collecting statistics on gangs through its National Youth Gang Survey. According to the latest survey, gangs exist all over the country, in rural, urban, and suburban areas. Big cities have the most problems with gangs: 86 percent of reported gang problems happened in large cities, such as New York and Los Angeles, while 14 percent happened in rural areas.

after his parents kicked him out for being expelled from middle school. He felt no one cared about him, let alone respected him—until he joined the Bloods when he was just 12 years old. "The Bloods just took me in. They didn't care about nothin' with grades or rules or chores. It was just all about makin' it [the gang] bigger, more powerful. I liked it. I felt important for the first time, man." However, as Big

Mike later learned, when a gang loses respect for a member, the

"The Bloods just took me in. They didn't care about nothin' with grades or rules or chores."

consequences usually include getting a severe beating or even being killed.

Protection and Violence

Another reason teens join gangs is to get protection from bullies or from other gangs. In fact 28 percent of kids who join gangs

The danger of violence between gangs is very real. A Houston, Texas, teen was killed when he and two of his fellow gang members were ambushed by about 20 members of a rival gang.

said they did so because they were afraid of someone at school. In some neighborhoods, getting this protection feels like a matter of life and death. Shaniqua comes from a neighborhood where gangs rule. She says the kids who try to stay neutral are harassed until they agree to join. She watched every day for six months as her brother and his friends were followed, made fun of, and finally beaten up until they agreed to join the gang. "I'm talking about 32- or 35-year-old O.G.'s [original gangstas] beatin' down on 14-year-olds," she says.

Still other kids approach a gang to ask for help defending themselves from another gang. A group of Cecí's girlfriends was stalked by a gang that cruised their street. Gang members drove back and forth, staring and scowling, trying to intimi-

Some Kids Just Wanna Have Bling

Some teenagers are motivated to join a gang because of the perceived perks that come with membership. Kids think that by joining a gang they will get money, bling, and live a party lifestyle. Randell grew up in a low-income neighborhood where gang style was everywhere. His family was

Gang members gain power by causing others to fear them.

date the girls. The girls were scared and felt they had no one to protect them. So they asked for protection from another well-known neighborhood gang, which agreed to help. The price? Membership, loyalty, and a willingness to follow orders.

poor, and he had to wear second-hand clothes from thrift stores. He was embarrassed and wanted to look as stylish as the Dip Set Purple-City gang members who roamed his neighborhood. So when the Dip Set offered him membership, Randell was quick to join. He says: "I didn't need no convincin'. The $300 Adidas on that boy who approached me did the sellin'. Yo, I was in." What teens like Randell don't realize, however, is that these "perks" are usually reserved for high-ranking members. It can take low-ranking members years of service to reap the material rewards of being in a gang, and by that point many are locked up, severely injured, or dead.

Gang members often find themselves serving time for the crimes they have committed.

Many famous hip-hop artists make gang life seem glamorous and exciting. But for most of these guys, their times in the limelight are cut short by prison or death. Rapper Snoop Dogg is known for being a member of the Crips, one of the most infamous gangs in the United States. He has been in and out of prison on drug, weapons, and violence charges. Tupac Shakur and Notorious B.I.G. have rapped about their gang affiliations and were killed in drive-by shootings. Both murders remain unsolved, though it's suspected that rival gangs, the Bloods and the Crips, were responsible for their deaths.

CHAPTER two

GETTIN' JUMPED AND THROWIN' SIGNS

Before they can be accepted into a gang, potential gang members must go through an initiation. Through this process, members prove they can follow orders, take a beating, and keep their mouths shut—sort of a test to see whether they will fit into the gang.

Initiation may include hurting an innocent bystander, committing a crime, getting beaten up—or worse.

Jumped In

The most common way of being initiated into a gang is to get "jumped in." Randell remembers when he was jumped in to the Dip Set Purple-City gang in Baltimore, Maryland. Gang leaders warned him that at some point, when he least suspected it, he would be jumped by five members of the Dip Set. "They told me almost everything. Who would beat me. How

The beating a person sustains when getting "jumped in to" a gang can leave permanent scars or even cause the person's death.

long it would last. That I couldn't do nothing to protect myself. That I might not live through it. They just didn't tell me when it was goin' down. So I was just always watching my back in those days," he says.

One day Randell was walking home from school when two boys grabbed him and dragged him into a yard where three other boys were waiting. "It was just like they said it would be—a 14-second beat down by five of their biggest gangbangers. They all pounded me at the same time. I just had to fall down and take it," he says. Since he took the beating "like a man," Randell was immediately accepted into the gang.

Another way to get initiated

Girls who join gangs face special risks during initiation. Besides the usual ways of proving themselves, girls face the potential for being "sexed in" to a gang. Cecí was forced to have sex with three male gang members for her initiation. "I mean, it was messed up," she says. "But at least I wasn't gangbanged [raped by several men at once] like some girls." Even so, girls like Cecí often end up with sexually transmitted diseases or pregnant, since male gang members rarely use protection. Cecí considers herself lucky, though, because "at least they didn't make me do it with none of them HIV boys. They do that, you know—to girls they don't like. They make 'em have sex with HIV positive boys. It's jacked up."

is to commit a crime for the gang. Big Mike was initiated into the Bloods in this way. He was ordered to rob a convenience store and turn the money over to gang leaders. "I never did anything bad like that before, so when they told me I had to knock off a store I was scared, man. They just said,

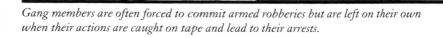

Gang members are often forced to commit armed robberies but are left on their own when their actions are caught on tape and lead to their arrests.

'Do it and you're in,' and gave me a gun," he says. Big Mike was told to choose a store in his neighborhood and rob the clerk at gunpoint. He was ordered to shoot anyone who tried to stop him. The store was empty and the owner cooperated, so Big Mike didn't have to use the gun. "I would've though," he says. "I mean, if the dude didn't give me the money. It's not like you have a choice. They just tell you what to do to get in and you do it."

Born Into the Life

Some kids are at high risk for joining a gang. For example, 90 percent of gang members in the United States are male, and four out of five gang members have a learning disability. Both statistics applied to Hugo, and his family was heavily involved in gangs. Hugo was "born into" the Norteños, a gang active in northern California. "My brother was already a member, and he was well-known, so, you know, I was just born into it." Hugo's initiation was confirmed when his brother was jumped in many years ago, when Hugo was still a small child. "My brother's initiation reputation was passed on to me. I was lucky. I didn't get no beat down or have to do a drive-by or nothin'."

Experts say that no matter how you get into a gang, the point of initiation is to prove to the other members that you are trustworthy and able to follow

"My brother's initiation reputation was passed on to me. I was lucky. I didn't get no beat down or have to do a drive-by or nothin'."

orders. From their very first day, members must be fiercely loyal and always protect the gang—no matter what.

Gang Life's True Colors

After initiation, gang members

show pride in their gang by wearing its uniform. This includes wearing or avoiding certain colors and sports team apparel. It also means dressing to the "left" or "right." For example, the official color for the Bloods is red, and for their rival gang, the Crips, it's blue. Depending on which gang you are in, you must wear your red or blue hat facing to the left or right. You also have to wear either your left or right pant leg rolled up, along with either the left or right side of your shirt collar.

George explains that after he was initiated, another gang member came to his house to scope out his closet: "The guy made two piles. He said, 'This stuff is fly, and this stuff is bye bye.'" George threw out any clothes with

Wearing the wrong colors or turning a cap to the wrong side can lead to serious injury or even death for gang members.

Tattoos give lots of information about the gang member wearing them and the gang he or she belongs to. For example, Bloods members have a "CK" tattoo that identifies them as "Crips killers." Crips gang members, on the other hand, have "BK" for "Bloods killers." Other tattoos use numbers, pictures, symbols, and letters to tell where the gang member is from, whether he or she has ever been to prison, and whether he or she has killed any rival gang members.

rival gang colors and bought several Houston Astros jerseys—his gang's favorite baseball team. George was told he could be killed for wearing the wrong colors or supporting a different team, which made it easy for him to throw out his old clothes. These strict dress codes help to establish an "us" and "them" mentality that is the foundation of how gangs operate—enemies and friends are easy to identify, said gang expert Tim Delaney.

After learning what to wear, George was taught how to communicate with his gang using codes, signs, and street names. He says of his education: "It was like learning a new language. They were like, 'You ain't George no more. Now you're G-Dog, and if you see the police shout out this, and if you see rival Gs [gangstas] throw your hands up like that.'" Gang members communicate with hand signs so that outsiders are

Gangs use numbers as part of their coded language. Some examples of how numbers are used to communicate or to identify a particular gang:

- 013 is used by the Bloods to tell its members to attack someone.

- 13 stands for "M," the 13th letter of the alphabet. It identifies someone as a member of the Southern California Mexican Mafia.

- 14 stands for "N," the 14th letter of the alphabet. It identifies someone as a member of Hispanic Northern California gangs.

- 187 is the California penal code for murder. Gang members use it as a threat, such as, "Keep walking or you'll find yourself 187ed."

- 5-0 refers to the police. The name comes from an old television show, *Hawaii Five-0*, but modern gang members use it to warn one another that someone is affiliated with the police, or that the police are on their way; 911 is also used to mean the police are on their way.

clueless as to what they are about to do. For example, George's gang has an elaborate set of signs they use just before attacking rivals. "Say we're on the street and a strange G comes through," explains George. "We all throw our sign at him. If he responds right, he keeps walking. If he responds wrong or throws a rival sign, we signal each other that it's on. There are no words—it's a completely silent judge, jury, and, sometimes, executioner."

George also learned that keeping the gang's secrets takes a lot of effort. In fact, secrecy is so tied up in gang respect and loyalty that many young gang

A gang member covered his face and flashed gang signs while he was being arrested.

members decide it's easier to let outside relationships go. "It's too hard, too confusing, to keep it all straight," says George. "Lying and covering up all the time is exhausting, man. For me it just got to the point that it was easier to let those on the outside of the life fall away."

CHAPTER three

TERRITORY AND LOOT: WHAT GANGS DO

Gangs work like a business. Their goals are to earn money and gain power. Unlike most businesses, though, they gain wealth and power through illegal, violent activities.

Gangs are willing to do just about anything to accomplish these goals—including commit crimes, sell drugs and weapons, and assault or even murder innocent bystanders and rival gang members. Even fellow gang members may be targets of brutal violence if they step out of line.

Tagging and Dissing

Graffiti, also called tagging, is how gangs mark the boundaries of their territory, and it's an important part of what gangs do.

21

The Crips have a huge membership, with "sets" in nearly every big city in America. Crips are so loyal to their gang, and they so hate the Bloods, that they refuse to use the letter B when writing, tagging, or speaking. Instead they cross out the B and insert the letter C when tagging or speaking words with B in them.

A public wall is painted by taggers every day.

Members spray paint pictures, words, and symbols on schools, bridges, fences, bus stops, street signs, and other highly visible areas to let others know it's their turf and to keep out. They also use tagging to issue threats to rival gang members. Julia is a tagger for her gang. She got the position when her gang's leaders decided she was a good artist. Julia explains: "They really liked the way I drew our name cuz I had style. So I was told to tag with the inside crew. It was cool. But there was a lot to learn."

Julia became the apprentice of a more experienced tagger. She spent hours a day learning her gang's geographical boundaries and codes. Sometimes she was ordered to issue threats to rival gangs with her graffiti. "If we was gonna hit a rival G, I'd put up a 782 [Florida's penal code for murder] next to the G's street name," she explains. "That was my job, man. I'd get my taggin' orders for the day and just hit the curb with it."

Julia also uses tagging to diss rival gangs. She and her team travel into enemy territory and draw over their rival's graffiti. In its place they paint their own gang's name and logo. According to Julia, "It sends a message that says 'We was here, right under your nose, and you didn't even know it, fools.'"

These missions are very dangerous because covering another gang's graffiti is considered seriously disrespectful. Julia's crew was once ambushed by another gang while painting over their graffiti. Julia got away,

The two uniting factors for all Bloods across the nation are their hatred of the Crips and their fierce loyalty to the United Blood Nation. This loyalty is reflected in the United Blood Nation Prayer, a pledge repeated by Bloods all over the country: "Will I ride? Yes I ride. Only because I bang with pride. When I die bury me 3 feet up with red on me. Rest in sleep, best believe I rest in the East. If I die in the street, don't forget to bang for me. If I live a G, won't forget the enemy. They lay out to rest hit 031 [code that means "I am Blood"] upon my chest."

23

but her fellow tagger wasn't so lucky. "I was paired up with this other girl," remembers Julia. "I heard them coming, so I ran, but she was too slow. I looked back one time to see they was pounding her. That girl was lucky they didn't kill her for what we done."

Stealing and Dealing

Increasing wealth is the driving force behind most gang violence and is the reason gangs commit a lot of their crimes. Gangs will sell merchandise, weapons, or drugs to bring in money and get members rich. Often the things sold by gangs are illegal or stolen themselves. Big Mike remembers an illegal gun deal that went down with his gang. "We sold some AK-47s, AR-15s, and handguns to this other gang who wasn't a threat to us. We made bank on

Gangs are often mixed up in the drug trade as well as other illegal activities.

that deal, but people definitely got hurt with them guns we sold."

Big Mike notes that gangs that sell weapons also tend to make money dealing drugs. He explains that gangs that deal drugs use guns to protect themselves from police, rival gangs, and thieves. When he was in the Bloods, kids called soldiers manned the corners in his neighborhood, selling crack and methamphetamine. "Drugs was where the money's at. We was dealin' in schools, on corners, in parks—wherever, man," he says.

Another way gangs make money is by simply taking it from others. Gang members often commit armed robbery to get cash or products, as Shaniqua knows from personal experience. She says her entire neighborhood shuts down at dusk for fear of being robbed. "Soon as the sun goes down, everyone gets off the street, cuz gangs be out looking for someone to rob," she says.

"They don't care if you carryin' a baby or walking your dog. You look like you got money, you gonna get hit. And stores? Forget it. All the clerks got cameras and guns and they hidin' behind bulletproof glass come nightfall." Sometimes gangs even break into private homes to steal

Gangs and gun violence were blamed for the increase in crime in the U.S. in 2006.

stereos, DVD players, computers, jewelry, and other valuables.

Gangs also make money by stealing and reselling cars. Stolen vehicles are driven to "chop shops," where they are stripped for their sellable parts. Hugo knows of a ring of car thieves that steals luxury cars from affluent neighborhoods. "They go after BMWs or Lexuses," he says. "They gots to be fast, though. These boys can get inside a car, start it, and drive it to a shop in less than 10 minutes." Once the cars are at the shop, gang-affiliated workers remove tires, stereos, batteries, carburetors, and any other valuable parts that the gang can sell.

Violence Reigns

Making money, committing crimes, and keeping tabs on who comes through your territory make gang life pretty stressful. Add violence to these activities and the life gets downright scary.

Randell says he developed severe anxiety from having to watch his back constantly. "It started the day I found out I was gonna be jumped in, and it never went away," he explains. "It feels like someone's always out to get me. Rival Gs, up and comin' young uns lookin' to make a name—I don't sleep but two hours a night, and I always got my hand under my pillow," where he keeps his

Mara Salvatrucha, also known as MS-13, got its start in El Salvador, but it's now one of the most violent gangs in the United States. MS-13 is known for committing murder, rape, and assault with a deadly weapon—as well as for carjacking and kidnapping its victims. With members in 42 states and in Central America, MS-13 is considered so great a threat to public safety that the FBI has created a special task force to destroy it.

The weak and vulnerable, including homeless people, are often the target of gang violence.

gun. Randell says violence is so normal in gang life that members become desensitized to it. "You see kids get beat and shot every day. It don't mean nothing to most Gs after a while."

George says he isn't worried about becoming a victim of gang violence as much as he is about being ordered to hurt an innocent person. George's gang is known for beating up neutral kids (kids who aren't in any gang) who are accidentally wearing the wrong colors while in his gang's territory. George says he can live with the idea that he might be killed, but he doesn't want to hurt an innocent person. "I chose this life, so I know sometime I'm gonna get hit. It's just a matter of time," he says. "What I'm not down with is hurting people on the outside who have nothing to do with the life. But it happens all the time in drive-bys, hold-ups, dares, and initiations. Bystanders got no idea how much danger they in at times."

CHAPTER four

WHAT'S THE WORST THAT COULD HAPPEN?

Joining a gang may seem like the answer to some of your problems, but it has serious consequences. Some consequences are short-term and personal, such as getting hurt, being forced to give up outside relationships, and being forced to do things against your will.

The long-term effects of gang membership are far worse, though. Gang members live every day with the threat of landing in jail or getting killed. Also, the minute you join a gang, you put your community and your family at risk for injury or death.

Communities in the Crossfire

It may seem weird to think that your decision to join a gang affects anyone but you—but it does. In fact, everyone in your community suffers from gang activity, whether it's

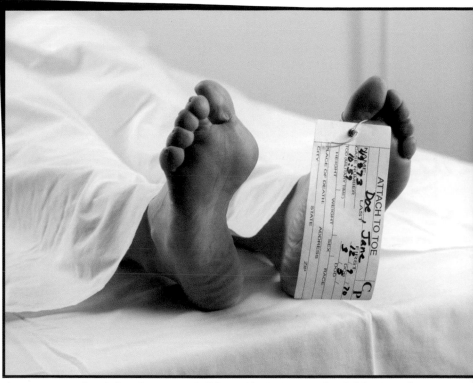

A recent survey found that 59 percent of all homicides in Los Angeles, California, and 53 percent of all homicides in Chicago, Illinois, involved gangs.

from crime, graffiti, or by becoming victims of gang violence. George recalls a time when people got hurt when members of his gang were ordered to carry out a revenge hit against a rival gang. Members drove by the second-in-command leader's house with orders to "shoot to kill." George wasn't prepared for what happened that day. He says: "Our boys rolled up and just started firing like they was told. Come to find out, it was the wrong house. Some young un got shot full of holes. Wasn't supposed to happen, but you know, civilians sometimes get caught up in the crossfire." Incidents such as these are a big enough problem that the federal government has set aside

An elderly victim of gang violence showed where a bullet pierced her window.

California has the largest gang population in the United States. There are believed to be 171,000 gang members in California, most of whom are 18 or younger. This results in a shocking mortality rate for young people in that state. In 2004, for example, gang violence was responsible for nearly 50 percent of the murders of people ages 19 through 29 and for 60 percent of the murders of people 18 or younger.

$2.5 million in grants for anti-gang programs in several major U.S. cities.

Communities suffer when innocents get caught in gang crossfire but are especially vulnerable when gangs select people at random to target. Hugo knows of a gang that initiates members by forcing them to attack and rob people. He explains: "They, like, tell their wanna-bes to just pick off some Joe at the bus stop or Jane walkin' her dog. They ruthless, man. They beat the hell out of some hook or rape some lady and steal all they can get. They gotta bring something valuable back to prove they did it."

It's almost impossible for people who live in a gang-infested neighborhood ever to feel safe. Mary lives in one such neighborhood. She's a single mom with two children and lives in fear that the neighborhood gang—a branch of MS-13—will either force her kids to join or kill them. "I try to keep my kids under their radar. I drive them to and from school, and they're not allowed outside after dinner—not even on our porch!" But Mary worries constantly that her sons will be hurt, killed, or inducted into

Wrong Place, Wrong Time

In June 2008, MS-13 gang member Edwin Ramos felt disrespected when local driver Tony Bologna prevented him from making a left turn down a narrow San Francisco street. Ramos opened fire on Bologna's car, killing the 48-year-old and his 20- and 16-year-old sons, who were also in the car.

The MS-13 gang marked a street sign to show the area is part of its territory.

31

the gang. She even decided to buy a gun, anticipating that her house will be robbed at some point. "These thugs don't care," she says. "They want something, they'll just take it! After two houses on my street were robbed, I got myself a gun—if they come in here, they're gonna get more than my TV!"

Doing Time

Since gangs make their money illegally and rule with violence, most members end up spending some time in prison. For petty crimes such as trespassing or graffiti, jail time is short—a few weeks or months here and there. Julia is just 13 years old,

When sentenced to prison, gang members form fierce alliances along racial lines to protect themselves and one another from rival gangs on the inside. Some of the most powerful—and violent—racially divided prison gangs include the Black Guerillas, the Mexican Mafia, and the Aryan Brotherhood. White gangs have the largest presence, according to a 2004 study conducted by the National Gang Crime Research Center. The study found 72.3 percent of U.S. prisons have whites-only gangs.

but she has already been locked up six times for minor offenses. Though she never spent more than six months at a time in a juvenile detention center, she says even just one night there is scary. "I did my time quiet like, but it wasn't easy. Most of them kids in juvy are gang-bangers and you have to represent or you get beat, or worse."

Gang members who commit assault, rape, and murder are likely to spend more time in prison than outside of it. Hugo knows this firsthand. Both of his parents are gang members who are serving life sentences in maximum security prisons. In fact, Hugo was born in a prison hospital and has never even met his father. His dad, "Chocko," was given a life sentence for the attempted murder of a rival gang member and the accidental murder of a bystander. Hugo says it was hard growing

up without parents. "It wasn't like I had my momma tucking me in at night. She got locked up before I was born for sellin' crack and MJ [marijuana]. It was her third strike, so, you know, she locked up for good, and I got no parents."

"I did my time quiet like, but it wasn't easy. Most of them kids in juvy are gangbangers and you have to represent or you get beat, or worse."

The Ultimate Price

Gang membership usually has tragic consequences for teens and their families, and too often members pay the ultimate price with their lives. Some teenagers die of fatal injuries after being jumped in, while others are killed in drive-by shootings. Some perish from drug overdoses. The circumstances of gang members' deaths may differ, but they all show that deciding to join a gang can be fatal.

Getting jumped in is often the first time gang members come

Drive-by shootings are a kind of hit-and-run tactic, in which a shooter fires from a moving or momentarily stopped vehicle. Sometimes gang members have an intended target, but often bystanders are hurt, too.

face-to-face with their own mortality. Some kids don't recover from the beatings they receive during their initiations, as was the case for 12-year-old Marco.

Marco was told he was getting jumped in by a group from La Nuestra Familia in Phoenix, Arizona. His brother, Vidal, begged Marco to reconsider. Vidal says: "I told Marco these boys was a bunch of savages. They're out for serious blood when they give someone a beat down." But Marco was committed to joining the gang and told Vidal it was "too late to stop it anyway."

Marco was jumped by four gang members on his way home from school. He was severely beaten for 13 seconds. That may not seem like much time, but it was long enough for members to pound him with their fists, elbows, and feet while he choked to death on his own blood. Vidal said his brother was unrecognizable at the hospital. "He had no face left, man. It was just pulp. His neck was broken. He had internal bleeding. The doctors said he died before they even finished beating him."

Vidal says he thinks in some ways his brother chose death because joining a gang means accepting the risk of getting killed. "You know what you're in for," says Vidal, "and ain't hardly nobody get out of that life alive."

Gang members often attend the funerals of friends who have died from gang violence.

QUIZ

Joining a gang has big consequences for you, as well as for your friends and family. Before you consider joining a gang, ask yourself these questions:

1. Am I willing to be jumped or sexed in?

2. Am I willing to stop talking to my friends who are not in the gang?

3. Could I hurt someone I don't know?

4. Do I want my family to be at risk for acts of gang retaliation or revenge?

5. Do I want to spend time in jail or prison to protect the gang?

6. Would I survive doing hard time?

7. Is there a career path I hope to take when I'm older?

8. Do I want to spend the rest of my life looking over my shoulder?

9. Would I want my little brother or sister to join a gang?

10. Is my life worth something to me?

CHAPTER five

GETTING OUT
AND MOVING ON

Getting out of a gang isn't easy. It's downright difficult and dangerous—and sometimes impossible to do without dying. After all, gangs operate within strict codes of loyalty and respect, and almost nothing violates those codes more than trying to leave the gang.

However, some gang members have been able to give up the life. They often get help from organizations devoted to supporting gang members who want to start new lives. It's necessary to have a plan, though—and to keep it a secret. Gangs don't want their members to leave and will do just about anything to prevent them from getting out.

Blood In, Blood Out

Some gangs have a "Blood In, Blood Out" policy. This means you must shed your own blood—or that of another

A YouthBuild USA class member (front) helped build a Habitat for Humanity home in Melbourne, Florida.

person—to get into a gang and to get out. For some gang members, BIBO ends in their own death or the murder of a loved one.

Big Mike was lucky enough to live through BIBO. When he was 17 years old, he refused to beat up a rival gang member. This was seen as dissing his friends, and he was jumped by six people from his own gang. After he was beaten up, Big

Mike decided to leave the gang. "After that, man, it was over. They didn't love me. They didn't respect me. To do me like that was wrong. After that, I was done."

It wasn't easy for Big Mike to leave, though. Gang leaders gave him a choice: get jumped out or sacrifice a family member. He recalls his final conversation with the head of his gang. "I said,

Just as when they are jumped in, people who want to leave a gang never know when they will be attacked.

lives with permanent scars across his face, chest, hands, and back—but is out of gang life for good.

Dressing Down and Easing Out

In gangs that don't have a BIBO policy, getting out takes time, patience, and a plan. Charles is a former gang member who worked with a counselor at his local YMCA to get out. Together they came up with a series of steps that would allow Charles to ease out of his gang. Charles explains how the plan took shape: "One day my counselor was like, 'It's gonna take six months to get you out safely, so you gotta have patience.' I just hunkered down and put my faith in the plan. It was all I had."

'That ain't no choice. Jump me out!' No way I was gonna let them touch my sister or anyone in my family. Someone had to give blood for me to go out, and it was gonna be me." Big Mike was brutally attacked once again by members of his own gang. He

Help is available for those who want to leave a gang. People such as Richard Trino Savala dedicate their time as gang counselors.

and rarely wore the clothing and colors that identified him as a gang member. He eventually stopped answering calls and text messages from gang members, saying he'd lost his phone.

After six months, Charles was out of the gang without having said a word to other gang members. He explains, "By that time, they was so used to me not being around and they was so wrapped up in their own business of making money they didn't give me a second thought. I was still cool with them, though, because I didn't make a big show of getting out. There was no disrespect or nothin'." Gang experts from various community and law enforcement organizations agree that Charles' plan was perfect

The first step for Charles was to spend less time with the gang. "At first, I was like, 'Yo, my mom is working a lot, and I gotta watch my little brother,' and then I joined up with a basketball team at the Y and said I had practice a time or two more than was factual." Charles spent most of his free time at the YMCA and got involved in a mentoring program for young kids. He started dressing in regular clothes because it put gradual distance between him and the gang.

New City, New Start

Other gangs would never allow members to ease out the way Charles did. At the first sign of pulling away, leaders often become suspicious. Cecí experienced this when she decided to leave her gang. She explains how vicious threats made by both female and male gang members prevented her from easing out. "They heard I wanted out, so they told me if I tried to leave they'd cut off my hands or kill my mom and sister. They said being sexed in wasn't nothing compared to what they'd do to me if I tried to leave. I was so scared. I felt sick all the time. But I wanted out so bad."

Cecí felt as if she had no options. But she knew she wasn't safe even if she stayed in the gang because they would never really trust her again. So she turned to the gang unit of the local police department and begged them to help her get out and to protect her family.

A gang unit investigator told Cecí the only way to be safe from revenge or retaliation from her gang was to move to another city, preferably in another state. "At first I was like, I guess I'm gonna

"They heard I wanted out, so they told me if I tried to leave they'd cut off my hands or kill my mom and sister."

die, cuz we can't afford to move to another state," Cecí said. "But then my mom was like, 'Baby girl, we gonna do whatever it takes to get you out.'"

The investigator working with Cecí's family put her in contact with Catholic Charities, a community-service organization that helped pay for the move. Still she had to be careful until all of the arrangements had been made. So Cecí stayed close to gang members and acted as if everything was normal. She

Across the country, police are trying to make a difference. Police in Anaheim, California, talked to students about the dangers of gangs.

attended meetings, went to parties, and pretended that her heart was still in the life. She made it known that her desire to get out was just a temporary bout of insanity.

Once she got the OK that it was time to leave, things happened quickly. Cecí, her sister, and her mom packed two bags each and took a taxi to the airport at 2 A.M. "The flight wasn't til 6 A.M., but we had to go when no one was up or watchin'," Ceci says. "We were all so scared and

The Los Angeles Police Department runs the Juvenile Impact Program, which prevents first-time youth offenders from getting stuck in the juvenile justice system and staying tangled up in gangs. Teenagers enrolled in JIP paint over graffiti, take self-esteem classes, and participate in "scared straight" programs. These are programs in which at-risk youth visit prisons and talk to inmates. The hope is that seeing the real-world consequences of crime, drugs, and gang life will help young people make better choices with their lives.

excited." Ceci says that when she stepped off the plane in her new town she felt relieved and could "finally take [a] breather from being scared."

A representative from a social service agency helped Ceci's family find an apartment. Soon after they moved in, Ceci's mom got a job and the girls enrolled in school. Ceci said, "Everything felt so normal after a while. I wasn't scared to be beat no more.

I was just a normal kid again—I could be anyone, do anything. It was a dream come true."

B.K. was a gangbanger in high school, but he wanted more out of life. He enrolled in community college and then transferred to the University of California in Los Angeles, where he is a pre-medical student. B.K. is excited about his future and says of college life: "Now I just go to school. Now I'm a Bruin."

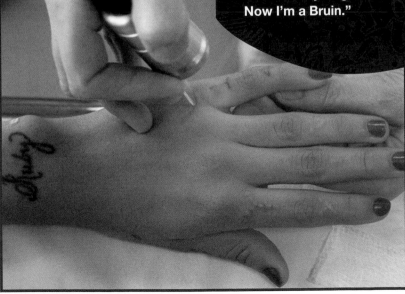

A former gang member underwent laser treatment to remove gang-related tattoos.

GLOSSARY

affiliation   connection to a gang

bling   shiny, flashy, and expensive pieces of jewelry

born in   inheriting gang membership from a family member

chop shop   illegal operation that breaks down stolen cars and sells their parts

diss   slang for disrespect

gangbanger   slang for gang member

hook   victim

initiation   rite of passage that must be completed before becoming a gang member

jumped in   method of gang initiation in which a person is beaten up by several gang members to prove he or she can handle the stress and violence of gang life

sexed in   method of gang initiation in which girls are forced to have sexual intercourse with several male gang members

soldier   gang member who works to increase a gang's wealth through criminal means

third strike   state law that automatically sentences an offender to a life sentence after being convicted of a violent crime for a third time

wanna-be   someone who hangs around a gang hoping to become a member

WHERE TO GET HELP

Bajito Onda Foundation
P.O. Box 270246
Dallas, TX 75227
214/275-6632
The Bajito Onda Foundation is a nonprofit group run by former gang members who help teenagers find alternatives to gang life. It offers job training and support to those who want to cut their gang ties.

Boys and Girls Clubs of America
1275 Peachtree St. N.E.
Atlanta, GA 30309-3506
404/487-5700
Boys and Girls Clubs of America are in many U.S. cities. Its programs strive to keep kids off the street while teaching them valuable life skills. Many clubs also provide gang intervention and prevention programs.

Council for Unity Inc.
50 Broadway, Suite 1503
New York, NY 10004
212/701-9440
The Council for Unity's mission is to empower youth and decrease violence in schools and communities. It offers information, programs, and assistance to kids and teens who want to avoid or leave gangs.

Gang Outreach Unit
270 S. Stone
Tucson, AZ 85701
520/351-4441
The Gang Outreach Unit is an organization within the Tucson Police Department. It works with the community to prevent kids from joining gangs by offering realistic alternatives.

YMCA of the USA
101 N. Wacker Drive
Chicago, IL 60606
800/872-9622
The YMCA is a national organization that offers many community development programs, including gang intervention and prevention. Representatives can answer questions or discuss concerns about leaving a gang.

SOURCE NOTES

Chapter 1

Page 5, line 5: George. Houston, Texas. Telephone interview. 14 Oct. 2008.

Page 8, column 1, line 2: Julia. Jacksonville, Fla. Telephone and e-mail interview. 25 Oct. 2008.

Page 8, column 1, line 19: Hugo. Oakland, Calif. Personal interview. 26 Oct. 2008.

Page 8, column 2, line 17: Big Mike. Oklahoma City, Okla. Personal interview. 14 Oct. 2008.

Page 9, column 1, line 7: Ibid.

Page 10, column 2, line 2: Shaniqua. Los Angeles, Calif. Personal interview. 14 Oct. 2008.

Page 12, column 1, line 1: Randell. Baltimore, Md. Telephone interview. 25 Oct. 2008.

Chapter 2

Page 13, line 21: Ibid.

Page 14, column 2, line 1: Ibid.

Page 15, sidebar, line 8: Cecí. Newark, N.J. Personal interview. 14 Oct. 2008.

Page 15, line 7: Big Mike.

Page 16, column 1, line 10: Ibid.

Page 16, column 2, line 1: Hugo.

Page 16, column 2, line 8: Ibid.

Page 17, column 2, line 23: George.

Page 18, column 2, line 6: Ibid.

Page 19, line 7: Ibid.

Page 20, column 1, line 2: Ibid.

Chapter 3

Page 22, line 19: Julia.

Page 23, column 1, line 12: Ibid.

Page 23, column 1, line 26: Ibid.

Page 24, column 1, line 2: Ibid.

Page 24, column 2, line 9: Big Mike.

Page 25, column 1, line 13: Ibid.

Page 25, column 1, line 25: Shaniqua.

Page 26, column 1, line 10: Hugo.

Page 26, column 2, line 3: Randell.

Page 27, column 1, line 4: Ibid.

Page 27, column 2, line 5: George.

Chapter 4

Page 29, column 2, line 1: George.

Page 30, line 12: Hugo.

Page 31, line 20: Mary. San Diego, Calif. Telephone interview. 1 Nov. 2008.

Page 32, column 1, line 4: Ibid.

Page 33, column 1, line 7: Julia.

Page 33, column 2, line 1: Hugo.

Page 34, column 1, line 11: Vidal. Phoenix, Ariz. Personal interview. 1 Nov. 2008.

Page 35, column 1, line 4: Ibid.

Page 35, column 2, line 5: Ibid.

Chapter 5

Page 38, column 2, line 2: Big Mike.

Page 38, column 2, line 12: Ibid.

Page 39, column 2, line 22: Charles. Albuquerque, N.M. E-mail interview. 1 Nov. 2008.

Page 40, column 1, line 3: Ibid.

Page 40, column 2, line 16: Ibid.

Page 41, column 1, line 14: Cecí.

Page 41, column 2, line 9: Ibid.

Page 42, line 12: Ibid.

Page 43, column 1, line 11: Ibid.

Page 43, sidebar, line 10: Jessica Lum. "After Gangs, Life Goes On." *The Daily Bruin*. 29 April 2008. 5 Feb. 2009. www.dailybruin.ucla.edu/news/2008/apr/29/after-gangs-life-goes/print/

Fiction

McDonald, Janet. *Brother Hood*. New York: Farrar, Straus and Giroux, 2004.

Myers, Walter Dean. *Autobiography of My Dead Brother*. New York: HarperTempest/Amistad, 2005.

Rivera, Louis Reyes, and Bruce George, eds. *The Bandana Republic: A Literary Anthology by Gang Members and Their Affiliates*. Brooklyn: Soft Skull Press, 2008.

Zephaniah, Benjamin. *Gangsta Rap*. New York: Bloomsbury, 2004.

Nonfiction

Donahue, Sean, ed. *Gangs: Stories of Life and Death From the Streets*. New York: Thunder Mouth Press, 2002.

Hagedorn, John M. *A World of Gangs: Armed Young Men and Gangsta Culture*. Minneapolis: University of Minnesota Press, 2008.

Savelli, Lou. *Gangs Across America and Their Symbols*. New York: Looseleaf Law Publications Inc., 2006.

Internet Sites

FactHound offers a safe, fun way to find Internet sites related to this book. All of the sites on FactHound have been researched by our staff.

Here's all you do:

Visit *www.facthound.com*

FactHound will fetch the best sites for you!

INDEX

ABOUT THE AUTHOR

Lauri S. Friedman earned her bachelor's degree in religion and political science from Vassar College in 1999. She is the founder of LSF Editorial, a San Diego writing and editing business. Friedman lives in San Diego with her husband, Randy, and their yellow lab, Trucker.

ABOUT THE CONTENT ADVISER

Billy AraJeJe Woods has a doctorate in psychology, a master's degree in education, and a bachelor's degree in psychology. He has been counseling individuals and families for more than 25 years. He is a certified transactional analysis counselor and a drug and alcohol abuse counselor. A professor of psychology at Saddleback College, Mission Viejo, California, Woods teaches potential counselors to work with dysfunctional families and special populations. He began his counseling career in the military, where he worked with men and women suffering from post-traumatic stress disorder. In his practice, Woods has worked with many young adults.